THE
SECOND
BEAST

By

WILL CLARK

The Second Beast

ISBN-13: 978-1514181430
10: 1514181436

Published By
Motivation Basics
P.O. Box 6327
Diamondhead, MS 39525

For more information visit the author at:
AuthorsDen.com

CONTENTS

Page

Introduction

An impending and prophesied disaster is about to occur in our great nation, while our national leaders do little to curtail its horrendous effects. To a large degree, however, their hands are tied to prevent that disaster. The president of the United States, Barack Hussein Obama, plays a major role to help create that devastation and he sits in an almost unchallengeable position.

He is identified in Revelation. Chapter 17, Verse 8 which reads, "...when they behold the beast that was, and is not, and yet is." He is described again in Verse 11, "And the beast that was, and is not, even he is the eighth, and is of the seven, and goeth into perdition." Could this describe the transition in Barack Obama's life? He was a Muslim, he is not a Muslim, and yet is a Muslim. Although coded, Islam is defined in Revelation as the 'Beast.' Major leaders within the Islamic Beast are described as 'horns.'

The Book of Revelation describes and prophesies many things and conditions. But, to understand those many things it's first necessary to find a code that will not only explain itself, but will also find keys to unlock other codes. This book will do that; find the keys to unlock many of those hidden codes.

The first clear and positive code discovered is the recognition of the

Christian religion in Revelation. That leads to the next code; the identification of the Islamic religion, described as the Beast, that Harlot of Babylon. In Chapter 17, Babylon, itself, is described as Islam, not the location of a physical bricks and mortar city.

The purpose for this book is not specifically to discuss religions. Religions themselves have no direct earthy consequences against others. Actions taken in the name of those religions are the devils, especially if they affect the lives of others who are the direct and negative targets of those religions; especially Islam. The purpose for this book is to uncover the codes that predict and identify a coming economic disaster that will cripple the United States as well as the rest of the world. It involves war in the Middle-East which will disrupt manufacturing, trade, transportation and food availability including within the United States. Life as we know it today will change. This is a political and survival question; not a religious question. Chapter 1 analyzes that first code; the identification of Christianity within Revelation.

Much of the information presented next is extracted from many of my other books; and from more current information found on the internet. The information is placed in an order that reveals the source and the danger to America; and to the world. Islam is the danger, the perpetrator, and the beast. Those who support the beast are just as guilty of danger and abomination as is that beast.

Chapter 1
The First Code
Christianity

There's a clear and definitive war against Christians and other related religions such as Jewish. In reality, this war taking place now is the same war prophesied in the Bible, in the Book of Revelation. That war is taking place before our very eyes as Islamic terrorists and other militants annihilate people and destroy lands and ancient artifacts while they raze humanity from the earth in their crazed rant in the Middle East and Africa.

Although their actions are crazed and inhumane, perhaps that might one day be curtailed. The devastating problem is the residual one; what happens to trade, commerce, food supplies and other sustenance throughout the world from the after effects?

This war was prophesied two thousand years ago by the Apostle John as he wrote the Book of Revelation while he was exiled on the island of Patmos. Patmos is still there in its same location just off the coast of Turkey. It's near the ancient city of Ephesus, one of the seven biblical churches, and the location where many of Jesus' disciples taught while that area was called Asia. Although cryptic, Chapter 12 in the Book of Revelation explains the beginning of this war on

Christianity and its cause.

Revelation begins with John's letters to the seven churches in Asia; which are: Ephesus, Pergamos, Laodicea, Thyatira, Philadelphia, Smyrna, and Sardis. These letters include a few coded words but not enough to hide the meaning of the admonitions and warnings. The surprise, after understanding more codes, is that those warning were also meant for Christians of today, not just at the time they were written. So, let's begin by unlocking the first - and primary - code in Revelation. It begins with the first verse of Chapter 12:

"And there appeared a great wonder in heaven; a woman clothed with the sun, and the moon under her feet, and upon her head a crown of twelve stars.

2. And she being with child cried, travailing in birth, and pained to be delivered.

3. And there appeared another wonder in heaven; and behold a great red dragon, having seven heads and ten horns, and seven crowns upon his heads.

4. And his tail drew the third part of the stars of heaven, and did cast them to the earth: and the dragon stood before the woman which was ready to be delivered, for to devour her child as soon as it was born.

5. And she brought forth a man child, who was to rule all nations with a rod of iron:..

6. And the woman fled into the wilderness, where she hath a place prepared of God,...

7. And there was war in heaven: Michael and his angels fought against the dragon; and the dragon fought and his angels,

8. And prevailed not; neither was their place found any more in heaven.

9. And the great dragon was cast out, that old serpent, called the Devil, and Satan, which deceiveth the whole world: he was cast out into the earth, and his angels were cast out with him.

13. And when the dragon saw that he was cast unto the earth, he persecuted the woman which brought forth the man child.

14. And to the woman were given two wings of a great eagle, that she might fly into the wilderness, into her place, where she is nourished for a time, and times, and half a time, from the face of the serpent.

17. And the dragon was wroth with the woman, and went to make war with the remnant of her seed, which keep the commandments of God, and have the testimony of Jesus Christ."

A summary: The known world at that time, primarily Rome, knew the Jews were expecting a messiah even before Jesus was born. They waited for him, and at the expected time had all newborn males killed hoping one would be that expected messiah. This mass killing is known as the 'Massacre of the Innocents,' by Herod the Great, the Roman appointed King of the Jews. It included the execution of all young male children in the vicinity of Jerusalem. "upon her head a crown of twelve stars" likely refers to the twelve Jewish tribes at that time.

Verse 14 seems most cryptic until 'two wings of a great eagle' is understood. Jews and Christians were totally persecuted until a 'great eagle' suddenly adopted Christianity as the world religion. Constantine the 'Great' who ruled from 306-337 adopted Christianity after a vision he had in 312 that he attributed to helping him win a great battle against a major enemy. It was the Battle of Milvian

Bridge.

According to writings, before the battle Constantine looked into the sun and saw a cross of light, with the words, "in this sign, conquer." He had his men paint a cross on their shields before the battle; that resulted in a major victory. As a result, he adopted Christianity for the Roman Empire. Soon afterward, his mother, Saint Helena, made many pilgrimage trips to the Holy Land identifying and preserving special Christian landmarks. This was the beginning of the Roman Catholic Church; 'where she is nourished for a time, and times, and half a time, from the face of the serpent.' Further information reconciles this time as 350 years.

What about the 'two wings of a great eagle?' These are the key words that allow important parts of Revelation to be interpreted. Without this understanding of Verse 14 nothing else makes any sense. An eagle with two widespread wings was the standard symbol for the Roman Empire. It was proudly carried on a tall staff ahead of marching troops; including King Constantine (two wings of a great eagle - Constantine the Great.)

This is the single most important clue to understanding the Book of Revelation. The prophesied dates and events are irrefutable.

Verse 14 presents critical information that explains events happening today, especially regarding the bloody tirade by radical Islamists throughout the world. It contains the words, "... where she is nourished for a time, and times, and half a time, from the face of the serpent."

This information is basically the key that unlocks two great mysteries. Considering this biblical information inside real-world history clarifies events that could not have been seen or interpreted much earlier than our present time. That time sequence could not have been interpreted before certain events happened. Now, they have happened and they can be interpreted..

By connecting and interpreting the information in Chapter 12, it's clear that the 'woman' described is a religion. And, that religion is Christianity. Once 'two wings of a great eagle' is interpreted, it becomes clear that Rome, Constantine at that time, protected that religion. The Roman Empire continued to protect that religion. But, what happened after the 'time, and times, and half a time?' The answer is unlocked with the keys of 'time.'

Constantine's battle at Milvian Bridge occurred in 312 A.D. It's reasonable to believe, after purges and indoctrination, Christianity became fully adopted within the Roman Empire approximately 350 A.D. which is the key to interpreting the times information; 'time, and times, and half a time.' In this case a time would be a hundred years. Addition of this information would indicate that total time must be 350 years. No other time suggestions are given. Since recorded history of that time is not precise (for example the exact date Christians came under the protection of Rome) approximations must be used for calculating.

Chapter 2
The Second Code
Islam

When did Islam become established? You guessed it; approximately 350 years later (another time, times, and half a time) after Rome adopted Christianity. Although Muhammad had his first vision that began Islam in 610 A.D. the religion didn't become fully established until much later, perhaps between 600 and 700 A.D. A formal date has never been established. Islam became a warrior class that began persecuting and killing Christians at that time.

Two points are critical here to identify Islam as the serpent that would attack Christians 350 years after Christianity was protected by Rome. The first point is the recognition of the 350 year identity time. Second is the introduction of the other woman, religion, also revealed in the Book of Revelation.

In summary, Rome gave protection to Christianity approximately 350 A.D.; Christians were attacked by another religion approximately 350 years later. But, who or what is that other religion? The Bible makes that answer absolutely and perfectly clear. It's identified in Revelation, Chapters 6 and 17. The description is a little lengthy, but I will include it here so it's not necessary to dig your Bible out of your closet. Let's begin with Chapter 17.

In the first verse an angel carries John, in the spirit, to show him the judgement of the 'great whore that sitteth upon many waters.' This was at the conclusion of several prophetic disasters. Verse 3 adds, "So he carried me away into the wilderness; and I saw a woman sit upon a scarlet coloured beast, full of names of blasphemy, having seven heads and ten horns." (The scarlet coloured beast is the rider of the red horse of the Apocalypse, when the second seal is opened.)

Verse 4 continues; "And the woman was arrayed in purple and scarlet color, and decked with gold and precious stones and pearls, having a golden cup in her hand full of abominations and filthiness of her fornication:" 5; And upon her forehead was a name written, 'Mystery, Babylon the great mother of harlots and abominations of the earth.' This information describes this woman as a respected religion, "arrayed in purple and scarlet colour." Purple is the color of royalty and respect.

Once it's understood that this woman, as was the first woman, is a religion, Verse 6 describes this religion: "And I saw the woman drunken with the blood of the saints, and with the blood of the martyrs of Jesus; and when I saw her I wondered with great admiration."

Is there any doubt in anyone's mind that this description could only be that of Islam? No other religion or group is "drunken with the blood of the martyrs of Jesus." That woman is the religion that's killing and beheading Jews, Christians, and anyone else in their path of destruction that refuses to accept their beliefs. This religion is clearly: Islam.

Now, for those who doubt the words of the Bible, and its prophesy, although the above information is clearly prophesy revealed in our

14

face, here's another item of Biblical interest. It pertains to what's happening today, even as we read and watch the news. Chapter 17 adds more. It explains another event to come; what happens to the 'mother of harlots - the whore;' those savage Islamic butchers.

When John wondered with 'great admiration' at the described woman, the angel asked why he marveled, then said he would explain more. Verse 7, "I will tell thee the mystery of the woman, and of the beast that carrieth her, which hath the seven heads and ten horns." Verse 9 adds, "The seven heads are seven mountains, on which the woman sitteth." (I now interpret these seven mountains as the seven continents upon which Islam has spread - not the seven hills of Rome as is so often discussed.)

Verse 12, "And the ten horns which thou sawest are ten kings, which have received no kingdom as yet; but receive power as kings one hour with the beast." That beast that will give them 'power' is not revealed; perhaps a provider of air strikes, manpower and logistics?

Verse 16 suggests the prophetic part. "And the ten horns which thou sawest upon the beast, these shall hate the whore, and shall make her desolate and naked, and shall eat her flesh, and burn her with fire." Does this not suggest that ten Islamic kings (they have already been identified) will battle the 'whore?'

The whore has already been identified as ruthless killers. Are there not ten Islamic countries now fighting against ISIS (radical Muslims) and other terrorists in the Middle East? If not prophetic, one must admit it's very interesting how closely the Bible describes what's happening today. And, Revelation was written by John 2000 years ago. The 'rider of the red horse' and the 'woman on a scarlet colored beast' have not one single prophesy of events to come that can be verified, as does the one 'who rides the white horse.'

15

Now, remember this quote above, "and I saw a woman sit upon a scarlet coloured beast, full of names of blasphemy, having seven heads and ten horns?" That woman was described again in Chapter 6, Verse 4; only this time the scarlet coloured beast was described as a red horse: "And there went out another horse that was red; and power was given to him that sat thereon to take peace from the earth, and that they should kill one another; and there was given unto him a great sword." Note the comment, 'and that they should kill one another.' At this very moment riders of the red horse (Muslims) are killing one another; they are killing other Muslims, the radicals, identified in Chapter 17 as the whore.

Does Islam have any prophesies revealed such as those from the Christian Bible? Absolutely not. It's only prophetic that the demonic actions by Islam are fully revealed in the Bible seven hundred years before Islam was founded. How did John know this would happen, and exactly when it would happen? He was shown it by a Devine Power.

How is that divine power of the Muslims demonstrated? Or, has it ever been demonstrated - except through threats, death, and physical conquest?

The information about the rider of the red horse was written shortly after Jesus was crucified. Christianity came under Rome's protection 350 years later (time, two times, and half a time.) After another 350 years, Islam was born from the moon god in Mecca. That's when Islam began having the 'blood of the martyrs of Jesus' on their swords.' If not, why does a crescent moon rise high atop their mosques?

Why was the second beast who told John to 'Come and see' when the second seal was opened, like a calf? Because in the end those who follow the rider of that red horse will be slaughtered like a calf by the

16

followers of the rider of the white horse.

The rider of the second horse, the red horse, has been revealed. That rider is the Islamic religion. That Islamic religion is determined to create abomination and destruction until the very end. It has nothing to do with religion and worship. It has everything to do with greed and the love of power.

Now that the two major characters, or forces, in Revelation have been identified, it helps explain other prophesies and information heretofore too coded to understand. The great war between these two forces; Good (rider of the white horse) and Evil (rider of the red horse) and Christianity and Islam, will be explained next.

Chapter 3
That Great Battle

As is the information about a single event scattered throughout Revelation, so is information about the great battle; commonly known as the 'Battle of Armageddon.' That's what has made reading of Revelation so difficult to interpret. It's not in the same place organized in a single sequence. The parts are scattered throughout the book. Now that we have the two parts identified; the protagonist and the antagonist, let's understand what happens relating to the white horse and the red horse.

Chapter 14, Verse 14 announces the preparation for that great battle. That preparation begins when a voice from heaven said, "And I looked, and behold a white cloud, and upon the cloud one sat like unto the Son of man, having on his head a golden crown, and in his hand a sharp sickle." Another angel came out of the temple and told the one riding the cloud to thrust in 'thy sickle, and reap; for the time is come for thee to reap; for the harvest of the earth is ripe.'

Verse 17 describes another angel that came out of the temple also having a sharp sickle. Verse 18 says another angel, which had power over fire, told that angel to, "Thrust in thy sharp sickle, and gather the clusters of the vine of the earth; for her grapes are fully ripe."

The next two verses give a brief conclusion, "And the angel thrust in his sickle into the earth, and gathered the vine of the earth, and cast it into the great winepress of the wrath of God. And the winepress was trodden without the city, and blood came out of the winepress even unto the horse bridles, by the space of a thousand and six furlongs." A furlong is approximately 220 yards, or one-eighth mile.

This review was that of a great battle. The intricacies and specific nature of the battle are scattered throughout in several chapters. It seems the warnings to the people of Islam, members of the woman, that religion that rides the scarlet colored beast, is given in Chapter 16 before the actual battle begins. The first verse says a 'great voice' told seven angels to 'go your ways, and pour out the vials of wrath upon the earth.' Ordinarily, the word 'great' indicates from Christ. These vials of wrath were warning for the people of the 'beast' to repent and turn from the beast.

These things John wrote in Revelation seem extremely harsh and possibly even not in understandable phrasing. The comparable series of events is also identified in Chapter 38 of Ezekiel. There the mention of blood, mountains, and shaking of the land is less detailed. Perhaps there were different interpretations of those events seen by John and Ezekiel. Nevertheless, they are quite similar. Chapter 16 describes what happens when the angels poured out the vials of the wrath of God upon the earth.

When the first angel poured out his vial upon the earth; 'and there fell a noisome and grievous sore upon the men who had the mark of the beast, and upon them which worshiped his image.' This mark of the beast was described in Chapter 13.

The second angel poured out his vial upon the sea ; 'and it became as the blood of a dead man; and every living soul died in the sea.' This seems extreme; however, it might not be as extreme as it sounds on the surface. Two things are not ordinarily considered. First, the word 'sea' ordinarily represents 'humanity' in Revelation. Secondly, 'soul' does not necessarily mean every person; only literally every soul. This likely has something to do with the first death and the second death of the soul; the second resurrection.

Verse 4 states that rivers and fountains of waters became blood when the third angel poured out his vial. The next verse indicates this is a judgment against those who have shed the blood of saints and prophets, and has given them "blood to drink," for they deserve that judgment. This likely is a response to the question asked when the fifth seal was opened, in Chapter 6. Verse 9 describes the sight of those souls slain for the Word of God. In Verse 10 they asked the question:

"And they cried with a loud voice, saying with a loud voice, How long, O Lord, holy and true, dost thou not judge and avenge our blood on them that dwell on the earth?"

Perhaps the indication of 'rivers and fountains of waters' does not suggest all rivers and fountains of waters 'became blood' only those concerning those to be avenged. Verse 7 supports this idea that this 'blood to drink' from their own deaths is appropriate judgment:

"And I heard another out of the alter (the alter above those who were slain) say, Even so, Lord God Almighty, true and righteous are thy judgments."

These verses related to judgments suggest those waters and rivers of blood would be only for that blood of judgment against those who have killed saints and martyrs of Jesus; not all rivers and fountains of waters. This same concept would apply to the second vial and the sea of blood, described above.

21

When the fourth angel poured his vial upon the earth, a clearer picture begins to emerge. It's a picture that shows how the first three events occurred and how they are directly related to warfare. It involves great heat when that vial is poured 'upon the sun.' Verse 9 continues with the results of that heat:

"And men were scorched with great heat, and blasphemed the name of God, which hath power over these plagues; and they repented not to give him glory."

This is a clear picture of warfare, even nuclear warfare. Although those followers of the beast, Islam, were again warned with great heat, from the power of God, they still refused to recognize that great Power. Not only does this 'great heat' describe a nuclear event; it also explains the 'noisome and grievous sore' from the first vial, and the vial to follow; the fifth vial. These are the results of radiation burn and cancers.

Verse 10 explains the results from the fifth vial, and is somewhat different from the others. Instead of the vial being poured 'upon the earth' it says, "upon the seat of the beast." It continues, "And his kingdom was full of darkness; and they gnawed their tongues for pain." But they still refused to repent even 'with their pains and their sores.'

Again, this does not describe a world event, only a location of the seat of the beast; most certainly somewhere in the Middle East, perhaps most likely Iran - but not necessarily. The beast's home base (seat) is in Mecca, which is in Saudi Arabia. Mention of the 'sores' again in this verse reinforces the idea of a nuclear event.

Pouring of the sixth vial is explained in Verse 12, "And the sixth angel poured out his vial upon the great river Euphrates; and the water thereof was dried up, that the way of the kings of the east might be prepared."

Verses 13 and 14 explain the preparation for the battle when, by working miracles, from the spiritual mouths of the dragon, the beast, and the false prophet, they gather for the great 'battle of that great day of God Almighty.' This includes 'unto the kings of the earth and of the whole world.' This appears a repeat scenario from Chapter 14, Verses 18 and 19, where an angel 'which had power over fire' telling another angel to 'Thrust in thy sharp sickle and gather the clusters of the vine of the earth; for her grapes are fully ripe.' In the previous two verses, the one who 'sat on the cloud thrust in his sickle on the earth; and the earth was reaped.' The two great forces are divided and prepared for battle.

In Chapter 16, Verse 15, God issues His final warning before that great battle, "Behold, I come as a thief. Blessed is he that watcheth, and keepeth his garments, lest he walk naked, and they see his shame." This warning is given for people to expect and plan for the coming horrendous events. This is the same warning that was given to one of the seven churches of Asia, Sardis; which will be detailed in the next chapter.

Verse 16 announces the final preparation for the great battle. It states, "And he gathered them together into a place called in the Hebrew tongue Armageddon." That's when the seventh angel poured out his vial into the air; "and there came a great voice out of the temple of heaven saying, It is done." The war begins in Verse 18:

"And there were voices, and thunders, and lightnings; and there was a great earthquake, such as was not since men were upon the earth, so mighty an earthquake, and so great."

Clearly, John's vision showed him nuclear war; that he could describe only as an earthquake - since he would not have known any other word for what he saw. Verse 19 adds, "and great Babylon came in remembrance before God, to give unto her the cup of the wine of the fierceness of his wrath." Babylon is defined in the next chapter as the Islamic religion. That information was presented earlier in Chapter Two in defining the Second Code.

The forecast of this great battle was given in Chapter 18, after the event itself is described in Chapter 16. That's what makes reading so difficult for many; it's not written in a direct and sequenced order. Regardless, let's see how the announcement of the battle actually matches the events of the battle. Verse 2 explains how Babylon has fallen to be so evil, "...is fallen, and is become the habitation of devils, and the hold of every foul spirit, and a cage of every unclean and hateful bird. 3, For all nations have drunk of the wine of her fornication, and the kings of the earth have committed fornication with her, and the merchants of the earth are waxed rich through the abundances of her delicacies." (Keep this in mind as we go to another chapter. 'waxed rich through the abundance of her delicacies' seems a minor point, but will be the basis of a major disaster to come to our great nation.)

Forecasts of the results from a fallen Babylon continue in Chapter 18. Verse 8 adds:

"Therefore shall her plagues come in one day, death, and mourning, and famine; and she shall be utterly burned with fire; for strong is the Lord God who judgeth her."

Will the major countries of the earth be satisfied when the great beast is destroyed by God's forces? That answer is: no. Verses 9-11 explains:

"And the kings of the earth, who have committed fornication and lived deliciously with her, shall bewail her, and lament for her, when they shall see the smoke of her burning, 10, Standing afar off for the fear of her torment, saying, Alas, alas that great city Babylon, that mighty city! For in one hour is thy judgment come. 11, And the merchants of the earth shall weep and mourn over her; for no man buyeth their merchandise any more." The next four verses give a long list of items no longer available for commerce. Verse 15 repeats their agony:

"The merchants of these things, which were made rich by her, shall stand afar off for the fear of her torment, weeping and wailing." This is the verse that explains the purpose for this book. Commerce and the availability of many items will not exist as we know it today. There will come a time of a failed commerce system, as it exists today, and of much famine throughout the world. This has been forecast and we have been warned, as in the warnings to the seven churches, "He that hath and ear, let him hear what the Spirit sayeth unto the churches." A review of John's letters to the seven churches in Asia will be reviewed next to emphasize that the information was not just for those seven churches; but to all churches and Christians throughout the whole world - today.

Chapter 4
The Seven Churches

Although there were more Christian churches at that time, John was instructed to write letters only to seven of those churches in Asia; that region now known as Turkey. Those were the churches at Ephesus, Sardis, Pergamum, Laodicea, Thyatira, Philadelphia, and Smyrna. Since the Book of Revelation is also called the Apocalypse, we should consider the possibility that information and those instructions aimed at those seven churches also apply to churches, Christians, even today. After all, the purpose for the book of Revelation is to give an overview of the end times.

What purpose would those letters serve if not as a warning for something to come - not something that had already happened at those seven churches? Let's review parts of those letters to see if any apply now; and if they warn us, today, of things to come.

Ephesus

John's first letter is to Ephesus. In Chapter 2 he writes, "Remember therefore from whence thou art fallen, and repent, and do the first works; or else I will come unto thee quickly, and will remove thy candlestick out of his place, except thou repent." In verse 7 he cautions, "He that hath an ear, let him hear what the Spirit saith unto the churches; To him that overcometh will I give to eat of the tree of

27

life, which is in the midst of the paradise of God."

Smyrna

His next letter is addressed to Smyrna. In this letter John lists some adversities of those citizens, then in Verse 10 writes, "...be thou faithful unto death, and I will give thee a crown of life." Again he adds, in Verse 11, "He that hath an ear, let him hear what the Spirit saith unto the churches; He that overcometh shall not be hurt of the second death." The second death can be understood by knowing the description of the first death. The first death includes the souls of those who are killed because they did not accept the 'mark of the beast' or worship the image of the beast. This is explained in Chapter 13: Verses15-18. The second death includes all others before and after that time. This is also known as the 'second resurrection' for those whose names are written in the 'book of life.'

Pergamos

The letter to Pergamos is similar to the others, but is somewhat different; as are all the letters somewhat different from the others. Verse 12 includes something new, "...These things saith he which hath the sharp sword with two edges." The sword has been mentioned before as coming from his (Christ's) mouth. From his mouth is not mentioned here. Verse 13 continues, "I know thy works, and where thou dwellest, even where Satan's seat is; and thou holdest fast my name..."

Pergamos, also called Pergamum by the Greeks, was the home of a famous medical center. It was dedicated to the Greek god of healing, named Asclepius. His symbol was the familiar serpent coiled on a staff that's still used today to represent medicine. The entrance to the medical center was decorated with a giant frieze of a serpent - which also represents Satan in the Bible. Hence, the 'seat of Satan.' Still, today, carved over the doorway are the words, "In the name of the gods, Death may not enter here."

The letter adds in Verse 17, "He that hath an ear, let him hear what the Spirit saith unto the churches; To him that overcometh will I give to eat of the hidden manna, and will give him a white stone, and in the stone a new name written..."

Barack Obama has a ring he has proudly worn for many years. He even wore it as his wedding ring. Although many, at first, claimed it was adorned with an Islamic inscription - that claim proved to be false. Upon further investigation what seemed an Islamic inscription was, in fact, two coiled serpents. He still proudly displays that ring; even as he announces great blessings of Islam.

Thyatira

An important part here begins with Verse 20, "Notwithstanding I have a few things against thee, because thou sufferest that woman, Jezebel, which calleth herself a prophetess, to teach and to seduce my servants to commit fornication, and to eat things sacrificed unto idols. 21, And I gave her space to repent of her fornication; and she repented not. 22, Behold, I will cast her into a bed, and them that commit adultery with her into great tribulation, except they repent of their deeds."

There is no specific reference as to the identity of this Jezebel. Gotquestions.org proposed one idea:

"After identifying Himself, Jesus affirms the church's positive actions: "I know your deeds, your love and faith, your service and perseverance, and that you are now doing more than you did at first" (Revelation 2:19). Five qualities are listed: 1) love, 2) faith, 3) service, 4), patient endurance, and 5) greater works.

Next, Jesus notes their sin: "Nevertheless, I have this against you: You tolerate that woman Jezebel, who calls herself a prophetess. By her teaching she misleads my servants into sexual immorality and the eating of food sacrificed to idols" (Revelation 2:20). Apparently, a false prophetess was leading believers into compromise. The church was engaging in sexual immorality and dabbling in idolatry. It is possible that "Jezebel" was her real name, but it is more likely the name was a metaphorical reference to the Jezebel of the Old Testament—another idolatrous woman who opposed God's ways. Rather than rebuke this false teacher and send her out of the church, the believers in Thyatira were allowing her to continue her deception.

Jesus pronounces judgment on this "Jezebel" and calls the church of Thyatira to repent of their sin: "I will cast her on a bed of suffering, and I will make those who commit adultery with her suffer intensely, unless they repent of her ways. I will strike her children dead" (Revelation 2:22-23).

Then Jesus encourages those who had remained faithful: "Now I say to the rest of you in Thyatira, to you who do not hold to her teaching and have not learned Satan's so-called deep secrets (I will not impose any other burden on you): Only hold on to what you have until I come" (Revelation 2:24-25). The faithful believers did not fall into Satan's trap, and they only needed to remain faithful until Christ's return." End of Gotquestions.org article.

Was this an admonition for the members of that specific church to "hold fast" or to members of all churches? Jesus used the identification; "that woman." Was this to identify another Jezebel - or the same woman identified in Chapter 17 "drunken with the blood of the saints?" Other information connects this possibility. This is from Wikipedia:

"Among the ancient ruins of the city, inscriptions have been found

30

relating to the guild of dyers in the city. Indeed, more guilds are known in Thyatira than any other contemporary city in the Roman province of Asia (inscriptions mention the following: wool-workers, linen-workers, makers of outer garments, dyers, leather-workers, tanners, potters, bakers, slave-dealers, and bronze-smiths)."

This is a description of the 'woman' in Chapter 17, Verse 4:

"And the woman was arrayed in purple and scarlet colour, and decked with gold and precious stones and pearls, having a golden cup in her hand full of abominations and filthiness of her fornication."

Perhaps Jesus was not speaking only and directly to that church in Thyatira. Could He also have been cautioning us about that 'woman' that threatens our salvation today with 'her' religion and that prophesy? Isn't the threat by Islam today exactly the same as the threat by that woman (religion) Jezebel? And, today we tolerate our 'Jezebel' the same as did the members of the church at Thyatira. We have been cautioned; who will listen?

In closing, the letter says, "But that which ye have already, hold fast until I come." Verse 29 adds again, "He that hath an ear, let him hear what the Spirit saith unto the churches." It doesn't say, "the Seven Churches."

Sardis

The letter to Sardis begins with another call to repent. Verse 3 continues, "If therefore thou shalt not watch, I will come on thee as a thief, and thou shalt not know what hour I will come upon thee." Verse 5 adds, "He that overcometh, the same shall be clothed in white raiment; and I will not blot out his name our of the book of life, but I will confess his name before my Father, and before his angels." Verse 6 repeats the admonition, "He that hath an ear, let him hear what the Spirit saith unto the churches." The white raiment and book of life was described earlier in this writing.

Philadelphia

After the introduction, Jesus says in Verse 8, "I know thy works: behold, I have set before thee an open door, and no man can shut it; for thou hast a little strength, and hast kept my word, and hast not denied my name."

Then he calls out the liars and hypocrites in Verse 9, "Behold, I will make them of the synagogue of Satan, which say they are Jews, and are not, but do lie; behold, I will make them to come and worship before thy feet, and to know that I have loved thee."

Verse 10 gives another strong clue that Jesus is speaking to everyone, in all times, when He says, "Because thou hast kept the word of my patience, I also will keep thee from the hour of temptation, which shall come upon all the world, to try them that dwell upon the earth."

Verse 11 repeats other warnings, "Behold, I come quickly; hold that fast which thou hast, that no man take thy crown." (Perhaps this crown is the one representing those who reign with Christ in Heaven during the Millennium period after the first resurrection.)

Verse 13, again, "He that hath an ear, let him hear what the Spirit saith unto the churches;" not just the seven churches of Revelation.

Laodicea

This is the church that was charged with being 'neither hot nor cold.' In the chapter, Jesus continued: Verse 19, "As many as I love, I rebuke, and chasten; be zealous therefore, and repent. 20, Behold, I stand at the door, and knock: if any man hear my voice, and open the door, I will come in to him, and have sup with him, and he with me. 21, To him that overcometh will I grant to sit with me in my throne, even as I also overcame, and am set down with my Father in his throne. 22, again, "He that hath an ear, let him hear what the Spirit saith unto the churches."

Summary

In summary, perhaps the warning to these seven churches to pay attention to events and listen to what the Spirit sayeth was not just for the seven churches. Too often the admonishment was repeated, "He that hath an ear" pay attention to what's happening - to current reality. It was repeated, and emphasized, for each of those churches - for every church. We are also told elsewhere in the Bible that when two or more people meet in God's name; there is a church. Therefore, we don't have to set foot inside a building called a 'church' to be warned.

At this time, and from these churches; what is our greatest warning from God in the Book of Revelation? To watch and to understand what's happening around us. He introduced us to that woman, Jezebel, as being in the church at Thyatira; but he didn't say who she was, and he didn't say she was not in other churches. Later, in Chapter 17 He showed us exactly who that Jezebel, religion, is. It's clearly the Islamic religion "drunken with the blood of the saints and with the blood of the martyrs of Jesus." That description could not be more clear and definitive.

We are warned not to be seduced by that 'prophetess.' Those who fall into her trap, or blindly turn aside and accept her ways, will be denied their salvation with God. That's why the Seven Spirits of God are within us; for power to defeat that great Beast and her Red Dragon.

John's writing in Revelation warns us of something more earthly and demanding while we are still here on earth; before that judgment day and before the resurrections. It will affect our physical well-being and our comfort and happiness. According to Chapter 18, Verse 11, "And the merchants of the earth shall weep and mourn over her; (when Babylon has fallen) for no man buyeth their merchandise any more:" This will be discussed in the next chapter.

Chapter 5
Warnings

The Book of Revelation is looked at and considered at length by many to be a warning to turn to God for salvation. Even many warnings in Revelation emphasize the first and second resurrections, and being judged from the Book of Life to determine each specific case.

In simple terms regarding this warning, God says to see and hear His Word for salvation, and not to be deceived to follow that Deceiver and Blasphemer empowered by Satan, that dragon, to choose another. When that Beast assumes more power over all people, it will be a death sentence to refuse his mark; to recognize and worship the Beast.

The other warning is for more earthly and physical purposes. It concerns commerce and availability of common items and food necessary for everyday life. Although the warning is directly at merchants, it will affect everyone alive at that time. This will be after all the devastation from the great war. And, a reference is hidden in the warning which might suggest the source of commodities and merchandise might be the lack of oil. To extract that hidden code, I must list several Bible references here to present that point. It might seem unnecessary to list all those here, but many people do not have a Bible; or know how to read and interpret a Bible. So, those many references are shown next; all in Chapter 18; after the Beast, Islam, is destroyed by those clothed in white raiment:

Verse 8: "Therefore shall her plagues come in one day, death, and mourning, and famine; and she shall be utterly burned with fire; for strong is the Lord God who judgeth her, 9, And the kings of the earth, who have committed fornication and lived deliciously with her, shall bewail her, and lament for her, when they shall see the smoke of her burning, 10, Standing afar off for the fear of her torment, saying, Alas alas that great city Babylon, that mighty city! for in one hour is thy judgment come.

Verse 11: And the merchants of the earth shall weep and mourn over her; for no man buyeth their merchandise any more; 12, The merchandise of gold, and silver, and precious stones, and of pearls, and fine linen, and purple, and silk, and scarlet, and all thyine wood, and all manner of vessels of ivory, and all manner vessels of most precious wood, and of brass, and iron, and marble, 13, And cinnamon, and odours, and ointments, and frankincense, and wine, and oil and fine flour, and wheat, and beasts, and sheep, and horses, and chariots, and slaves, and souls of men. 14, And the fruits that thy soul lusted after are departed from thee, and all things which were dainty and goodly are departed from thee, and thou shalt find them no more at all.

Verse 15: The merchants of these things, which were made rich by her, shall stand afar off for the fear of her torment, weeping and wailing. 16, And saying, Alas, alas that great city, that was clothed in fine linen, and purple, and scarlet, and decked with gold, and precious stones, and pearls!

Verse 17: For in one hour so great riches is come to nought. And every shipmaster, and all the company in ships, and sailors, and as many as trade by sea, stood afar off, 18, And cried when they saw the

36

smoke of her burning, saying What city is like unto this great city!

Verse 21 reemphasizes the severity of damage done to those areas of the beast: And a mighty angel took up a stone like a great millstone, and cast it into the sea, saying, Thus with violence shall that great city Babylon be thrown down, and shall be found no more at all. Verse 22 confirms that saying, "And the voice of harpers, and musicians, and of pipers and trumpeters, shall be heard no more at all in thee; and no craftsman, of whatsoever craft he be, shall be found any more in thee; and the sound of a millstone shall be heard no more in thee;"

It seems most strange that a large list of items no longer available from the beast is presented in such a manner in the Bible. Why would those who survived and 'became rich' from the products of the Beast be so concerned? After reading that list many times, over two years, an important clue finally emerged. Finally, I observed two items out of place or not properly presented in that list. And, the same event occurred twice; which meant it was not by accident the first time.

Verse 12 lists several items within a certain identification. Then it mentions two: purple and scarlet, without a noun, or a subject. They are just colors presented as an object. Verse 16 repeats that same identification of; purple and scarlet, without an object to identify; just colors. At first, it just seems like something misplaced; but twice? So, I researched further.

I found that amber is the natural color of oil. I also discovered that red is the mother color of purple. Amber is the natural color of oil; and amber comes in shades of amber, red, and purple. This identification strongly supports the idea that John was describing oil as the basis of commerce in Babylon, that Islamic Beast world. Why did he use the identifications of 'scarlet and purple' instead of oil? Because he had no idea what it was when he saw it; it was only something scarlet and purple. It was another 1900 years before it had a name; oil.

With that color code, the identity of Babylon is once again reinforced in Verse 16. In summary, verse 16 says that great city (Babylon) was clothed in fine linen (the fabric of the wealthy and influential) based on riches of purple and scarlet (oil) and they flaunted their gold and precious stones upon themselves. Absence of these things made rich men weep and wail, for they knew it was the basis of their trade and commerce. The absence of those things, especially oil, that allows some to grow rich, will cause those with those high expectations to weep and wail. But what about others of the earth who merely go from day to day trying to survive? Will they suffer as harshly as those who hope to get rich and wealthy?

So, what connects this beast, this Islam, with the rider of the horse in Chapter 6? Verse 4 states that, "was red: and power was given to him that sat thereon to take peace from the earth, and that they should kill one another; and there was given unto him a great sword." Chapter 17, Verse 3 connects everything, "So he (the angel) carried me away in the spirit into the wilderness; and I saw a woman sit upon a scarlet coloured beast, full of names of blasphemy, having seven heads and ten horns."

To briefly summarize; the rider of the red horse is the same rider, the woman (religion,) who sits on the scarlet coloured beast. That scarlet color represents power in resources, especially oil. That religion has without question taken peace from the earth with all its murdering and slaughtering of innocent humans, including young children. That religion has a 'great sword' to take peace from the earth and it does so with inhuman atrocities. The religion itself is completely based on 'blasphemy,' whereby one claimed to take the place of Christ; the Antichrist. Otherwise, there is no foundational principle that established that 'religion.'

Now that the source of great problems and tribulations are exposed, how will that affect those common citizens of earth who merely want to go about their daily lives, not involved with any of these religions or politics? They will be as harshly effected as those who suffer those great atrocities.

Understanding how devastating the results of that great battle will be, everyone on earth will be effected. Life as we know it will change; and it will be mostly from the loss of normal commerce and transportation. Shortages of food in many places will cause much famine; lack of common supplies and tools will cripple industry, and insecurity on major highways will curtail transportation access that we consider normal today. Let's consider a few possible examples; and according to information in Revelation, the situation could be even much worse than in these examples:

First, let's consider food. Much of our stable vegetable, fruit, and nut supply traditionally came from California. Today, much of our food comes from Central and South America. Whether it comes from California or South America it requires an integrated transportation system to disperse it all over the United States. Consider what would happen if:

1. Oil from the Middle East suddenly ceased?

2. Integrated parts for manufacture or repair of food production, farm, equipment were not available because manufacturers lacked energy to produce those parts?

3. The price of available oil doubled or tripled due to demand and availability, making transportation of food unprofitable?

4. Petroleum products and other chemicals and fertilizers were not available, or could not be delivered, to feed and nourish local food growth?

5. Cattle feed could not be distributed due to lack of dependable transportation, or it couldn't be produced and cultivated?

6. Workdays were limited to daylight hours due to lack of fuel to produce enough electricity; that available energy source would have to be allocated to higher priorities?

7. Food required to be refrigerated for transportation or storage could not be preserved in that environment?

8. Enough energy was not produced, or was not timely effective to allow safe storage in home refrigerators or freezers?

9. Mechanical farm equipment, including harvesters and pickers, was not available to process food from the ground, stalk, or trees?

10. Grain elevators and other mechanized storage facilities did not have energy to load, protect, and dispense those stored products?

That absence of oil from the Middle East (or the distribution and delivery thereof) would have many other devastating affects world-wide that can't be anticipated at this time. The reference below mentions ships and the sea, but the connotation of 'sea' in Revelation also refers to 'sea' of people and humanity; therefore consider major highways as part of that sea.

Revelation specifically mentions shipping and ship masters in Chapter 18. Verse 17 begins that specific identification: "For in one hour so great riches is come to nought, And every shipmaster, and all the company in ships, and sailors, and as many as trade by the sea, stood afar off, 18, And cried when they saw the smoke of her burning,...19...wherein were made rich all that had ships in the sea by reason of her costliness! For in one hour is she made desolate."

Not only would a lack of or shortage of oil affect shipping; the absence of the ability to process and manufacture items when delivered would curtail much shipping. Many places of the whole world would become 'desolate.'

Famine would become a major problem throughout the whole world. Many parts of Africa that traditionally suffer famine would have the 'death of humanity and beasts' strewn about for hundreds of square miles, or more.

Survival would once again become the nature of humanity. Prosperity and comfort would be abandoned and forgotten. Perhaps those in the 'sea' identified as 'preppers' are the ones most prepared according to the warnings; and there are two clear and distinct in Revelation.

First is the warning to the Church at Sardis (all churches):

"Be watchful, and strengthen the things which remain, that are ready to die; for I have not found thy works perfect before God. Remember therefore how thou hast received and heard, and hold fast, and repent. If therefore thou shalt not watch, I will come on thee as a thief, and thou shalt not know what hour I will come upon thee."

Second is that final warning in Revelation Chapter 16, Verse 15:

"Behold, I come as a thief. Blessed is he that watcheth, and keepeth his garments, lest he walk naked, and they see his shame."

At this point, one must ask why Barack Obama and his administration criticize preppers and others who read and trust the words of the Bible as 'dangerous right-wing nuts.' Why does he, and others who follow him, worship him, and promote his principles of Islam and anarchy despise and reject those led by the principles long ago written in the Bible - from experiences through much shed blood? Why are they so fearful of, and so viciously attack that Word of God?

And we very seriously must ask: Why does Barack Obama so adamantly refuse to allow development of our own abundant supply of oil and other natural resources to alleviate these hardships when they begin? What is his purpose for refusing us security? Does he know something; and is supporting it?

Why does Barack Obama follow and promote the principles of a self-proclaimed prophet who has no ancestral history of struggle for a divine vision. That self-proclaimed prophet demonstrated only a lust for power; that power gained through war, physical conquest, murder, and fear. Where and when does that religion he created show love, tolerance, compassion and understanding for its fellow humanity who choose otherwise?

It claims to be a 'religion of peace.' In this case, peace is an unusual and strange word; perhaps following in the case of the 'strange god' mentioned in Daniel, Chapter 11, Verse 39:

"Thus shall he do in the most strong holds with a strange god, whom he shall acknowledge and increase with glory: and he shall cause them to rule over many, and shall divide the land for gain."

Could this, in any way, describe the actions and intentions of Barack Obama? How and why would he 'divide the land?' Let's examine that question in the next chapter.

Chapter 6
Dividing Us

Has anyone in the history of the United States done more to divide our great nation, the United States of America, than Barack Hussein Obama? Absolutely not. Is he a patriot; a normal average citizen; or a traitor to all we hold dear and precious in our short-lived land? That answer has not presented itself yet, but perhaps we will have that answer sometime in the near future.

Perhaps his actions detrimental to the continuation of our great nation as we know it and as we hope it will always be are intentional; or perhaps by inexperience and fallacy. Let's consider one of those possibilities with an old quote from Marcus Tullius Cicero, 58 B.C. in his speech in the Roman Senate:

"A nation can survive its fools, and even the ambitious. But it cannot survive treason from within. An enemy at the gates is less formidable, for he is known and carries his banner openly. But the traitor moves amongst those within the gate freely, his sly whispers rustling through all the alleys, heard in the very halls of government itself. For the traitor appears not a traitor; he speaks in accents familiar to his victims, and he wears their face and their arguments, he appeals to the baseness that lies deep in the hearts of all men. He rots the soul of a nation, he works secretly and unknown in the night to undermine the pillars of the city, he infects the body politic so that it can no longer resist. A murderer is less to fear. The traitor is the plague."

Would Barack Obama make any attempt to divide us and our land? Are there any indications or suggestions of that possibility? Absolutely; and without any doubt whatsoever. He has divided our land and our great people within three dimensions. One is by religion; one is by respect for our nation; the other is by economic status. Let's consider them separately, beginning with religion:

Historically, America has been known as a 'Christian' nation. We have been proud and honored to be seen under that umbrella of love, support, tolerance, respect, and support to our fellow man. This is how those of us who understand salvation see ourselves. What was one of the first things Obama said about Christians?

In his 2006 speech to a liberal Christian group, then Senator Barack Obama said: "Whatever we once were, we are no longer a Christian nation - at least, not just. We are also a Jewish nation, a Muslim nation, a Buddhist nation and a Hindu nation, and a nation of nonbelievers."

Many people have analyzed these comments, and many have suggested he meant to include other religions as being part of our nation. Nevertheless; he clearly stated the words, "Whatever we once were, we are no longer a Christian nation." By itself, this could have been considered just a random misquote or a random mistake. But, too many other comments support his direct comment that we are no longer a Christian nation. Possibly what he meant to say was, "When I'm finished we will no longer be a Christian nation; we will be a Muslim nation." All indications suggest this was his meaning.

On June 28, 2006, during his 'Call to Renewal' speech, he mocked three sections of the Bible, including the Sermon on the Mount, which he called 'so radical.' He asked, mockingly, "Can either of these be used to guide public policy?" Here is that unedited part of the speech mocking the Bible:

"And even if we did have only Christians in our midst, if we expelled every non-Christian from the United States of America, whose Christianity would we teach in the schools? Would we go with James Dobson's, or Al Sharpton's? Which passages of Scripture should guide our public policy? Should we go with Leviticus, which suggests slavery is ok and that eating shellfish is abomination? How about Deuteronomy, which suggests stoning your child if he strays from the faith? Or should we just stick to the Sermon on the Mount, a passage that is so radical that it's doubtful that our own Defense Department would survive its application? So before we get carried away, let's read our bibles. Folks haven't been reading their Bibles."

How would one who blasphemes the Bible know what's in the Bible? Furthermore, why would someone who refuses to salute our flag, appropriately, use the Bible to try to prove a political point. Is that, in itself, not blasphemy?

During Obama's remarks at a San Francisco fund raiser in April, 2008, he attempted to explain the resentment of many citizens in small towns in Pennsylvania. He stated, "

"You go into these small towns in Pennsylvania and, like a lot of small towns in the Midwest, the jobs have been gone now for 25 years and nothing's replaced them. And they fell through the Clinton administration, and the Bush administration, and each successive administration has said that somehow these communities are gonna regenerate and they have not. And it's not surprising then they get bitter, they cling to guns or religion or antipathy toward people who aren't like them or anti-immigrant sentiment or anti-trade sentiment as a way to explain their frustrations."

Again, this is another negative comment about America, American citizens, and Christianity - which forms the major principles of our country's foundation. His comment shows contempt to Americans, and it demonstrates further blasphemy against God. Although in his admonition to those citizens he does not specifically say "Christians." That is, nevertheless, the religion to which he refers.

In that short statement he criticized Clinton, Bush, and others who shared an interest in trying to improve people's lives. Then he blames their attitudes and opinions on personal characteristics. In his short statement, he equates guns, religion, prejudice (antipathy toward people who aren't like them) Hispanic haters (anti-immigrant sentiment) and anti-trade sentiment (against foreign competition) as an evil embodiment of those citizens. In other words: their attitude is their problem. Does this show love and respect for America and Americans and its Christian values?

On April 16, 2009, he required the monogram for the name of Jesus be covered before he made his speech at Georgetown University. The monogram above an archway was covered with black painted plywood. Certainly he would not consider this blasphemy against God and the Bible, or an insult to America, whose charter and pledge recognize God as part of our heritage and culture. Does that action by Obama demonstrate his love and care for America and his respect and support of Christianity?

What is Obama's attitude toward Islam? Let's let his comments speak for him directly. These are reported by Joshua Riddle, October 2, 2013, through youngcons.com. The article is titled: Forty mind-blowing quotes from Barack Obama about Islam and Christianity:

1. "The future must not belong to those who slander the Prophet of Islam."

2. "The sweetest sound I know is the Muslim call to prayer."

3. "We will convey our deep appreciation for the Islamic faith, which has done so much over the centuries to shape the world — including in my own country."

4. "As a student of history, I also know civilization's debt to Islam."

5. "Islam has a proud tradition of tolerance."

6. "Islam has always been part of America."

7. "We will encourage more Americans to study in Muslim communities."

8. "These rituals remind us of the principles that we hold in common, and Islam's role in advancing justice, progress, tolerance, and the dignity of all human beings."

9. "America and Islam are not exclusive and need not be in competition. Instead, they overlap, and share common principles of justice and progress, tolerance and the dignity of all human beings."

10. "I made clear that America is not – and never will be – at war with Islam."

11. "Islam is not part of the problem in combating violent extremism – it is an important part of promoting peace."

12 "So I have known Islam on three continents before coming to the region where it was first revealed."

13. "In ancient times and in our times, Muslim communities have been at the forefront of innovation and education."

14. "Throughout history, Islam has demonstrated through words and deeds the possibilities of religious tolerance and racial equality."

15. "Ramadan is a celebration of a faith known for great diversity and racial equality."

16. "The Holy Koran tells us, 'O mankind! We have created you male and a female; and we have made you into nations and tribes so that you may know one another.'"

17. "I look forward to hosting an Iftar dinner celebrating Ramadan here at the White House later this week, and wish you a blessed month."

18. "We've seen those results in generations of Muslim immigrants – farmers and factory workers, helping to lay the railroads and build our cities, the Muslim innovators who helped build some of our highest skyscrapers and who helped unlock the secrets of our universe."

19. "That experience guides my conviction that partnership between America and Islam must be based on what Islam is, not what it isn't. And I consider it part of my responsibility as president of the United States to fight against negative stereotypes of Islam wherever they appear."

20. "I also know that Islam has always been a part of America's story."

From comparing his comments about the two religions, can anyone even imagine he is other than a Muslim? Would any reasonable person believe him when he says he is a Christian? Have you ever heard of the word, 'Taqiyya?'

Taqiyya is Muslims' authorization and duty to lie to infidels (non-Muslims) in order to camouflage Islam's holy war strategy to conquer the world. Muslims are allowed to lie and to deceive to promote their religion.

Obama has proven many times to be a blasphemer, to criticize Christianity; he has also proven many times to be a deceiver, one who avoids the truth when it damages his agenda. Consider his comments regarding the Benghazi attack; where he said it was caused by reaction to someone's video. He knew that was not the truth when he said it. Also, "If you like your doctor, you can keep your doctor." He knew that was false when he announced it. To use words from Revelation: he is a 'Deceiver and a Blasphemer.'

He also divides our nation by his leadership away from respect and love of our great nation. One of his first actions as president was to apologize to the world for our past mistakes and transgressions. Why did he do that; what was the purpose, other than to create that division? Let's itemize a few of those announcements with his intent to degrade our nation:

1. Apology to the Muslim World. President Obama, interview with Al Arabiya, January 27, 2009.

"My job to the Muslim world is to communicate that the Americans are not your enemy. We sometimes make mistakes. We have not been perfect. But if you look at the track record, as you say, America was not born as a colonial power, and that the same respect and partnership that America had with the Muslim world as recently as 20 or 30 years ago, there's no reason why we can't restore that."

2. Apology at the G-20 Summit of World Leaders. News conference by President Obama, ExCel Center, London, United Kingdom, April 2, 2009.

"I would like to think that with my election and the early decisions that we've made, that you're starting to see some restoration of America's standing in the world. And although, as you know, I always mistrust polls, international polls seem to indicate that you're seeing people more hopeful about America's leadership.

I just think in a world that is as complex as it is, that it is very important for us to be able to forge partnerships as opposed to simply dictating solutions. Just to try to crystallize the example, there's been a lot of comparison here about Bretton Woods. "Oh, well, last time you saw the entire international architecture being remade." Well, if there's just Roosevelt and Churchill sitting in a room with a brandy, that's an easier negotiation. But that's not the world we live in, and it shouldn't be the world that we live in."

3. Apology to France and Europe. Speech by President Obama, Rhenus Sports Arena, Strasbourg, France, April 3, 2009:

"We must be honest with ourselves. In recent years we've allowed our alliance to drift. I know that there have been honest disagreements over policy, but we also know that there's something more that has crept into our relationship. In America, there's a failure to appreciate Europe's leading role in the world. Instead of celebrating your dynamic union and seeking to partner with you to meet common challenges, there have been times where America has shown arrogance and been dismissive, even derisive."

4. Apology before the Turkish Parliament. Speech by President Obama to the Turkish Parliament, Ankara, Turkey, April 6, 2009.

"Every challenge that we face is more easily met if we tend to our own democratic foundation. This work is never over. That's why, in the United States, we recently ordered the prison at Guantanamo Bay closed. That's why we prohibited--without exception or equivocation--the use of torture. All of us have to change. And sometimes change is hard.

Another issue that confronts all democracies as they move to the future is how we deal with the past. The United States is still working through some of our own darker periods in our history. Facing the Washington Monument that I spoke of is a memorial of Abraham Lincoln, the man who freed those who were enslaved even after Washington led our Revolution. Our country still struggles with the legacies of slavery and segregation, the past treatment of Native Americans.

Human endeavor is by its nature imperfect. History is often tragic, but unresolved, it can be a heavy weight. Each country must work through its past. And reckoning with the past can help us seize a better future."

5. Apology for U.S. Policy toward the Americas. Opinion editorial by President Obama: "Choosing a Better Future in the Americas," April 16, 2009.

"Too often, the United States has not pursued and sustained engagement with our neighbors. We have been too easily distracted by other priorities, and have failed to see that our own progress is tied directly to progress throughout the Americas. My Administration is committed to the promise of a new day. We will renew and sustain a broader partnership between the United States and the hemisphere on behalf of our common prosperity and our common security."

6. Apology to the Summit of the Americas. President Obama, address to the Summit of the Americas opening ceremony, Hyatt Regency, Port of Spain, Trinidad and Tobago, April 17, 2009.

"All of us must now renew the common stake that we have in one another. I know that promises of partnership have gone unfulfilled in the past, and that trust has to be earned over time. While the United States has done much to promote peace and prosperity in the hemisphere, we have at times been disengaged, and at times we sought to dictate our terms. But I pledge to you that we seek an equal partnership. There is no senior partner and junior partner in our relations; there is simply engagement based on mutual respect and common interests and shared values. So I'm here to launch a new chapter of engagement that will be sustained throughout my administration."

7. April 20, 2009, CIA Headquarters, Langley, VA:

"So don't be discouraged by what's happened in the last few weeks. Don't be discouraged that we have to acknowledge potentially we've made some mistakes. That's how we learn. But the fact that we are willing to acknowledge them and then move forward, that is precisely why I am proud to be President of the United States, and that's why you should be proud to be members of the CIA."

8. Apology for Guantanamo in Washington. President Obama, speech at the National Archives, Washington, D.C., May 21, 2009.

"Unfortunately, faced with an uncertain threat, our government made a series of hasty decisions. ... I also believe that all too often our government made decisions based on fear rather than foresight; that all too often our government trimmed facts and evidence to fit ideological predispositions. Instead of strategically applying our power and our principles, too often we set those principles aside as luxuries that we could no longer afford. And during this season of fear, too many of us — Democrats and Republicans, politicians, journalists, and citizens — fell silent. In other words, we went off course.

There is also no question that Guantanamo set back the moral authority that is America's strongest currency in the world. Instead of building a durable framework for the struggle against al Qaeda that drew upon our deeply held values and traditions, our government was defending positions that undermined the rule of law. In fact, part of the rationale for establishing Guantanamo in the first place was the misplaced notion that a prison there would be beyond the law--a proposition that the Supreme Court soundly rejected. Meanwhile, instead of serving as a tool to counter terrorism, Guantanamo became a symbol that helped al Qaeda recruit terrorists to its cause. Indeed, the existence of Guantanamo likely created more terrorists around the world than it ever detained."

9. May 3, 2013 in Mexico:

"Our attitudes sometimes are trapped in old stereotypes. Some Americans only see the Mexico that is depicted in sensational headlines of violence and border crossings — and let's admit it. Some Mexicans think that America disrespects Mexico, or thinks that America is trying to impose itself on Mexican sovereignty or just wants to wall ourselves off. And in both countries, such distortions create misunderstandings that make it harder for us to move forward together. So I've come to Mexico because I think it's time for us to put the old mind-sets aside. It's time to recognize new realities, including the impressive progress of today's Mexico."

These are only a few representative examples of what Obama really thinks about the United States and our heritage. He lists our mistakes and apologizes for his vision of our shortcomings. He has never spoken of all the good America has done for the world. That list would be endless.

It includes the sacrifice of our soldiers in two world wars. Thousands of patriotic soldiers, airmen and sailors lost their lives storming the beaches to rescue Europe from the evil grasp of the Axis powers. Thousands gave their lives on the beaches on the first day - during only a few hours.

America has given billions of dollars all around the world to help improve people's lives, even much of that money to many countries who hate us and would do us harm with only a little provocation. Does Barack Obama remind those countries he visits of those deeds and sacrifices of America? No! He condemns and criticizes America for what he perceives as ignorance, weakness, and lack of concern for other countries. He is a president of the United States. He should know better; he should demonstrate at least a touch of respect for our nation and its history. He does not.

Obama has exibited genius in dividing our nation economically. He has pitted the wealthy and successful against the poor and less successful in our society. He has convinced many of the less successful that their lack of success and happiness has been caused by 'greedy rich people.' He has spewed that mantra so many times and so successfully that he has a great following. Even as great as his herd of sheep is now, he spurns our Constitution by inviting millions of illegal aliens to come into our country; not bringing their skills and contributions to make America better, but instead to cross our borders with their hands held out for all the free things he offers them.

Of course our history has been a 'nation of immigrants' and we have welcomed them for centuries. The difference this time, however, is that they are not coming here to offer their efforts and talents to make themselves and their families successful and prosperous, and to add to the over-all well being of our nation - they are coming to take what they can get; what Obama promises they will get. Welfare payments, food stamps and other free support have never been so high in our nation. What happens when those demanding 'free stuff' far outnumber those who can pay for those free things?

The result will be exactly what Barack Obama has planned. Our nation will be divided for his gain, as he supports that 'strange god' mentioned in Daniel. Can you even imagine what would happen if Obama garners all that support and loyalty he craves and needs to fulfill his final objective with America? But what is his real objective? For certain, it's not to help make America a better place. Could it be that objective identified in Revelation, Chapter 13?

Chapter 7
Mark of the Beast

Chapter 13 in Revelation is the one that describes the 'mark of the beast' and the 'second beast' identified otherwise as the 'False Prophet.' After an introduction in the first verses, verse 11 begins the introduction of the second beast, "And I beheld another beast coming out of the earth; and he had two horns like a lamb, and he spake as a dragon." The next three verses describe this second beast as having the same power as the first beast, and does great wonders such as 'making fire come down from heaven on the earth in the sight of men.' By these miracles he deceived men to make an image to the first beast 'that had the wound by a sword, and did live.'

Verse 15 says he had power to give life unto the image of the beast that he might speak. He added that those who would not worship the image of the beast should be killed. Today, of course, any image can be made to speak by use of computers and holograms.

Verse 16 begins, "And he causeth all, both small and great, rich and poor, free and bond, to receive a mark in their right hand, or in their foreheads." This is that 'mark of the beast' that's so often mentioned. By correlating these two descriptions of a mark and a seal in their foreheads, it's likely that an actual mark or seal is not placed on one's forehead. Perhaps that simply means that one accepts in his or her mind (brain, thoughts, forehead) that religion or that thought.

In the case of the 'mark' it could even be a number such as a credit card number, or a universal serial number given to every follower of the 'beast.' That number could be 'remembered' in the forehead; or it could be on a card carried and presented in the 'right hand' such as a credit card or any other identification card that's presented today. In either case, one will be required to have this number to transact any financial business. Those others will either have provisions to last 42 months during the 'abomination of desolation,' grow their own food (and other necessities of life,) survive in the wilderness, or they will be beheaded as martyrs of Jesus.

If, as interpreted previously in this writing, Muslims are the followers of the 'beast,' that 'Mother of harlots,' then Muslims will be the only ones having that mark of the beast described in Chapter 13. Perhaps a timely example of this mark on the forehead involves how people are selected for murder and beheading now in Africa and the Middle East. When many people are captured by the radical Muslims (identified otherwise as the 'whore,') they can often save their lives by proving they are Muslim. They do this by quoting verses from the Koran. If they quote from their foreheads 'their minds and memory' is this not a mark on the forehead? If they can't, many are then beheaded.

Perhaps at this time we must consider a very critical point, or question regarding the mark of the beast. The question has never been asked, "Which beast?" Is the mark of the beast from the first beast, or from the second beast often called the False Prophet? Two points strongly suggest the mark is demanded by the second beast - the supporter of the first beast.

The first beast has long been dead; that's why the second beast required an 'image to the beast which had the wound by the sword,

58

and did live' be made by those who dwell on the earth. Muhammad died in 632. (Verse 14-15)

Second, the second beast has access to modern technology and modern warfare that the first beast did not have - as in his miracles of fire from the sky. And, if the first beast were still alive, why would it be necessary to build an image of that beast to worship? It wouldn't be necessary - his followers could just worship the live real first beast. But, who or what was that first beast with the 'wound by the sword and did live?'

Perhaps Muhammad's battle of Uhud gives a clue. This is from one Muslim writing about that battle: "In the battle of Uhud, March 19, 625, when his Makkan enemies attacked the Muslims, Prophet Muhammad suffered a head injury and his front teeth got smashed." Most historians suggest the battle was caused by and initiated by Muhammad. (Onislam.net; Prophet Muhammad: Master of Tolerance, by Raya Shokatfoard, Freelance Writer, Jan. 6, 2014.)

This is another account from another Muslim writer: "The Prophet lost the day and very nearly lost his life. He was struck down by a shower of stones and wounded in the face by two arrows, and one of his front teeth was broken."

This historical information strongly suggests the 'first beast' has come and gone. Possibly the second beast, also known as the false prophet, exists today, since the time is ripe for that nuclear attack prophesied when the seventh seal is opened. Barack Obama and his administration are now in negotiations with Iran concerning that nuclear possibility. The negotiations, at this time, are not to stop it.

Verse 18 in Chapter 13 perhaps describes the second beast instead of the first beast, as often identified as the Antichrist in other parts of the Bible. Perhaps the Antichrist existed in 625 A.D. describing himself as a Prophet replacing the role of Jesus. The word 'antichrist' does not mean against Christ; it means 'in the place of Christ.' Muhammad was replacing Christ as the true Prophet - so he and his followers claimed.

Verse 18 describes the name of the second beast: "Let him that hath understanding count the number of the beast; for it is the number of a man; and his number is Six hundred threescore and six." (666) Describe someone today, in a high position, that strongly supports Islam and has the power to 'maketh fire come down from heaven on the earth in the sight of men.' That's the name of the man with 18 letters in his full name. It's written in Verse 18.

The question becomes, how extensive is the inclusion of this mark of the beast. Is it only in the lands that were considered the world that John knew at that time? Or will the second beast become so dominant that all the world will be included?

At this time, one must believe that all the world as we know it now will not be included with the mark. Of course, all the world will be affected by the results of the opening of the fifth seal where there will be much economic despair, starvation; and the sixth seal, because economic shortages resulting from lack of oil and open shipping lanes will restrict many. The integrated economic system and processing will not operate as a well-oiled machine as it does today. According to the Bible, it will be a time of great tribulation; especially during the 42 months of the Abomination of Desolation.

Through John's vision, Christ warned two times to 'those who have an ear' to listen to the warnings and be prepared. He will come as a thief to eliminate the two beasts and the red dragon from the earth. Perhaps that second beast exists today and is now scheming to take his place alongside the beast and the dragon. How and when will we know? Revelation describes him as a 'blasphemer and a deceiver.'

Who do we know today who solidly fills that description; with a strong tendency to support and promote that first beast?

Conclusion

The Seven Spirits of God must be understood in regard to current events, those things happening around us and to us in light of us being in the image of God. Satan has always waged war against God, beginning with Adam and Eve in the Garden of Eden. That war has never stopped. Satan will never be fulfilled until every man and woman follow his evil dictates and persuasions. In waging war against God, in effect Satan wages war against us who are made in the image of God. Through His grace, God has given us, his followers, those Seven Spirits to stand guard against and deny the force and influence of Satan.

Yes - those Seven Spirits are within us - because we are made of and from God. His Spirit lives within each of us making us, those who believe, His 'Temple.' He said it, so it must be Truth. Each person must understand those Spirits and that relationship to reach eternal salvation, and to allow others the opportunity to reach that salvation in His light.

That opportunity is quickly being eroded by current events, worldly matters, and the eventual full empowerment of the beast. Should we stand by, wring our hands in agony, and accept the inevitable as the Will of God? Or should we activate and use those Seven Spirits to defeat Satan and his plan for tribulation and conquest of humanity and the human spirit?

God said he would conquer with a 'two-edged' sword. Does that mean we should keep our swords 'sheathed' or since we are, as He said, the image of God, should we use our swords in that same battle against Satan? God said he would win that battle in the end; should we not be there raising our real swords in victory as He sits on His throne after that great battle? Those in white clothing who helped fight that battle will be there with Him to celebrate that great victory. That is His word. His word will last forever and forever.

Satan is not an idle bystander. He is constantly seeking to turn the world with all its inhabitants against God. He will soon empower the beast, that Islamic religion, to help him reach that goal. At this time, that beast has not been given his great authority and power, but that time seems near; perhaps too near. Let's review some tactics and influences Satan is using to accomplish that final goal. First, is his war against Christians; the remnant of her seed.

This modern war against God and Christianity began creeping forward in America in the 1950s - 1970s with the emerging atheist movement. During the late 1940s until the 1950s most Americans still felt blessed with the hand of God carrying them safely through the Second World War. Americans led the way to preserve world freedom and hope; that hope being accepted as a special gift from God. Those Seven Spirits: Power, Strength, Wisdom, Riches, Honor, Blessings, and Glory, were within us through that horrific world-wide danger.

During this brief period, very few openly expressed a disbelief in God. When the few who did, they were frowned upon as having no respect for humanity. America was proudly a Christian nation. Our presidents and other senior leaders openly expressed our nation's belief in God and Jesus, and their guiding hands for our generous humanity and great prosperity.

This war was openly announced in America when Barack Obama forcefully proclaimed to a liberal Christian group in 2006, "We are no longer a Christian nation." Although he added in that speech after he said, "We are no longer a Christian nation - not just," the intent was very clear. His intention was to express that America would no longer be guided by Christian principles and concepts; those which had guided the formation and development of a great and Godly nation guided not only by Biblical principles but also by humane principles of a caring society.

Did Barack Obama have a serious and determined background against Christianity when he made that statement, "We are no longer a Christian nation?" Perhaps this war had already been predetermined when he wrote in his book, 'Audacity of Hope': "I will stand with the Muslims should the political winds shift in an ugly direction."

The war against Christians became even more blatant and obvious when God was openly denied three times at the 2012 Democratic National Convention. By voice vote of the entire assembly, they rejected placing God's name in their party platform; many from the floor even booed and mocked the proposal. Perhaps this three times denied activity has another prophetic origin announcing the war against God and Christianity - remember Peter's three denials when asked if he knew Jesus?

Now that war against us has two clear and distinct fronts. One is on the battlefield with knives, guns, bullets, and explosives. This is identified as terrorism. It's purpose is to inflict fear and physical subservience. This front is real, and openly exists even now in the United. States. Brandon Walker from In News, reported on July 30, 2014 in an article titled: '22 Jihad Training Camps in the US - FBI Refuses to Take Action.' The article reveals:

"There are over 22 confirmed terrorist Jihad camps in the United

65

States belonging to Jamaat ul-Fuqra, a Pakastan Muslim Brotherhood and Al Qaeda related branch. Now a combined media effort, we find police officers working to double as the compound militia. To top it off, the FBI states that their hands are tied in monitoring their activities despite a training video that is years old, possible murders, and proof of illegal activities."

The second front is more subtle and insidious. While the world is distracted with Islamic terrorism, others with deliberate and planned purpose undermine and erode our Christian freedom from the inside, in accordance with that Islamic Memorandum describing the 'Silent Jihad.' Perhaps Cicero's speech in the Roman Senate in 58 B.C. should be considered in our present time.

Another Important Consideration is the identity of the antichrist, identified in Revelation as the beast; and our comparative time associated with the beast.

So, Who is the antichrist or who will become the antichrist? How can he be identified? Perhaps these verses give a clue. He can be identified by his great deceptions and blasphemies:

2 John 1:7 - For many deceivers are entered into the world, who confess not that Jesus Christ is come in the flesh. This is a deceiver and an antichrist.

1 John 2:22 - Who is a liar but he that denieth that Jesus is the Christ? He is antichrist, that denieth the Father and the Son.

Mark 13:22 - For false Christs and false prophets shall rise, and shall shew signs and wonders, to seduce, if it were possible, even the elect.

2 Thessalonians 2:3-12 - Let no man deceive you by any means: for that day shall not come, except there come a falling away first, and

that man of sin be revealed, the son of perdition.

Luke 21:8 - And he said, Take heed that ye be not deceived: for many shall come in my name, saying, I am Christ; and the time draweth near: go ye not therefore after them.

Matthew 24:24 - For there shall arise false Christs, and false prophets, and shall shew great signs and wonders; insomuch that, if it were possible, they shall deceive the very elect.

Daniel 11:21 - And in his estate shall stand up a vile person, to whom they shall not give the honour of the kingdom: but he shall come in peaceably, and obtain the kingdom by flatteries.

How will the beast gather such a large following that he will go forth 'through peace, conquering?' That answer is partially given in Daniel 11. It begins with Verse 33, "And they that understand among the people shall instruct many: yet they shall fall by the sword, and by flame, by captivity, and by spoil, many days. 34, Now when they shall fall, they shall be holpen with a little help; but many shall cleave to them with flatteries." 35, "...even to the time of the end: because it is yet for a time appointed." 36, And the king shall do according to his will; and he shall exalt himself, and magnify himself above every god, and shall speak marvelous things against the God of gods." 39, Thus shall he do in the most strong holds with a strange god whom he shall acknowledge and increase with glory; and he shall cause them to rule over many, and shall divide the land for gain."

So, how could this happen? How could someone divide the land for his gain? Perhaps an answer is suggested in other references. It begins in 2 Thessalonians, Chapter 2. Verse 17 begins, "Comfort your hearts, and stablish you in every good word and work."

This word, 'work' could be interpreted in many ways, but another reference clears up that confusion. The next clarity begins with Chapter 3, Verse 6, "Now we command you, brethren, in the name of our Lord, Jesus Christ, that ye withdraw yourselves from every brother that walk disorderly, and not after the tradition which he received of us. 7, For yourselves know how ye ought to follow us; for we behaved not ourselves disorderly among you; 8, Neither did we eat any man's bread for naught; but wrought with labor and travail night and day, that we might not be chargeable to any of you; 9, Not because we have not power, but to make ourselves an ensample unto you to follow us."

Verse 10 begins a stronger case for work, "For even when we were with you, this we commanded you, that if any would not work, neither should he eat. 11, For we hear that there are some which walk among you disorderly, working not at all, but are busybodies. Verse 12 summarizes their idea, "Now them that are such we command and exhort by our Lord Jesus Christ, that with quietness they work, and eat their own bread."

And, we shouldn't forget 1 Corinthians 3:7, "So then neither is he that planteth any thing, neither he that watereth; but God that giveth the increase. 8, Now he that planteth and he that watereth are one; and every man shall receive his own reward according to his own labour. 9, For we are labourers together with God; ye are God's husbandry, ye are God's building."

In summary, this explains how one might divide the land for his gain. Barack Obama is a gifted expert in this process. He encourages many not to work, not to prosper, not to fulfill their responsible and biblical tasks by refusing to work for their own bread. He encourages them to be 'disorderly' and wait for others to give them their bread through more taxes that can be aimed at welfare, food stamps, more fatherless babies, and self-imposed total despair.

This 'dividing the land for his gain' eliminates those he casts down to despair from ever finding the Grace and Light of God. By his actions with them, and their ready acceptance of getting something without effort, he condemns their souls to disorder and into the waiting hands of Satan. And, having growing support with increasing followers following his 'great words and blasphemies' what might become the final result of his plans and actions? He 'divides the land for his gain.' That's why it's so important to understand what's taking place today.

Since many ideas and references have been presented in this writing, perhaps this book should close with a brief summary of the key points to explain how the references are related. Let's begin by showing the chain reaction of relationships.

The code is broken by first uncovering the concept that the first woman mentioned in Revelation as in pain with a child to be delivered was Christianity. She was identified as Christianity when in 350 A.D. Constantine the Great (two wings of a great eagle) protected her, then formed the Roman Catholic Church. (Time, times, and a half time 350 years.)

That safety net ended after another 350 years. That's when Muhammad began forming the Islamic religion before 700 A.D.; and began slaughtering Christians and others under the guise of killing only for the purpose of defense. History proves he murdered many by self-initiation to fulfill his prophesies of having a world where only Muslims existed. He called himself a prophet, taking the place of Christ; and his followers believed him and supported him. That's the purest definition of an 'antichrist.' This concept is further verified by the fact that Muhammad suffered a mortal head injury from which he recovered. This was prophesied in Revelation 700 years before it happened. Since then, the Beast (Islam) has continued to wage war against Christians; the 'remnant of her seed.'

Islam fulfills the general identification of the 'Beast' throughout Revelation. It was prophesied that 'through peace he shall conquer many.' Islam vehemently claims it is a religion of peace which is one of the greatest deceptions of mankind. Still, today, Islamists are slaughtering thousands of innocents, especially in the Middle East and Africa.

The rider of the 'red horse' is clearly and without any doubt the Islamic religion. In the description of the rider of the red horse it says, "and that they should kill one another." Chapter 17 reveals Islam as Babylon, the mother of harlots. One harlot is the 'whore' who occupies the position of murderer and terrorist. Verse 16 says the ten horns (Islam) will attack the whore and make her desolate. This repeats the description of the rider of the red horse that 'they should kill one another.' That's exactly what's happening today - as I write these words. The Islamic nations (Babylon - the Beast) are attacking the terrorists; at the moment primarily that whore ISIS.

The Antichrist, that First Beast, is dead - Muhammad. Things that are to occur will be led or influenced by the Second Beast; the False Prophet who will support and promote that first beast. Who in our world today expresses such love and adoration toward the Islamic religion? Who in our world today has enough authority and influence to create the 'mark of the beast' and make those other prophesies happen? Only one man; and you know his name. His full name, in accordance with Chapter 13, Verse 18: has 18 letters.

We Christians have been told what will happen to our future. We have also been told that we must hold fast, or we will suffer the same consequences as those who follow that Beast, and his name; and that Jezebel. And, we have also been given the Seven Spirits to overcome those difficulties we must face in the future. We have been given Knowledge, Wisdom and Power. We share those things with a loving God who protects us, and with all the saints and martyrs who have gone before us. Those seven spirits are universal gifts to all who understand and accept; and that's really easy - since we all share the same Spirit in the same universe forever and forever.

Based on all this information and all these warnings, perhaps one caution should be added at this point and under events happening as I write this. Barack Obama has created another separation; a great divide that's most dangerous. His leadership has created an environment of distrust toward those appointed to protect us, and those of his sheep who are growing through his power and influence.

Our leaders at the highest levels must never allow him to create such a division in our society that he will justify martial law for himself with our police forces and our military. Most certainly, that will be the great power granted to him by the red dragon. We have been warned many times in Revelation. We have been warned not to destroy ourselves.

God bless and protect us all.
We have been warned.

About The Author

Will Clark's author experiences began by writing inspection and evaluation reports in the U.S. Air Force. He is a retired Air Force officer and a Vietnam veteran, serving in Saigon from 1966 to 1967. His other overseas assignments include Misawa, Japan and Ankara, Turkey. He taught on-base college courses while stationed in Turkey.

In 1995, as a 'Friends of Education' study skills project, he authored a book, *How to Learn*, to encourage students to improve their grades in DeSoto County, Mississippi. Education supporters printed and distributed four thousand copies. The following school year he wrote a weekly education column for a local newspaper, *The DeSoto County Tribune*. He also taught an adult GED class. His book, *How to Learn*, has been updated and is now available everywhere.

His next published book was *School Bells and Broken Tales*, a parody of nursery rhyme characters, also a motivation and education book for children. Other books include *Shades of Retribution,* a historical novel, and *Simply Success*, a motivation guide for students and employees.

His action novel, The Atlantis Crystal, is the first of a trilogy based on Atlantis and crystals. The other two books are: *She Waits in Atlantis*, and *Return to Atlantis*. This trilogy is based on his travels while assigned to Turkey, site of the ancient city of Troy. His latest political thriller is: *America 20XX: The New World Order.*

He is a past member of Toastmasters, a life member of Optimists International, a past Optimist Club president, and a past Optimist area lieutenant governor.

For more information about the author, visit:
AuthorsDen.com

Things We Must Never Forget
Until We Know All the Answers

Benghazi

Why were four Americans killed?
Where was Hillary Clinton while it was happening?
Where was Barack Obama while it was happening?
Why did they lie and blame the event on a video?
Why were rescuers on 'stand by' told to 'stand down?'

Fast and Furious

Who authorized the operation?
Why did the operation continue after weapons were lost?
Why did the procedure have no procedure?
Why weren't tracking devices used?

The IRS Scandal

What was the highest level involved?
Who initiated it?
Why hasn't anyone been fired or reprimanded?
What dangers could be unleashed by this organization?

Greatest Quotes
of
Our Time

Michelle Obama
February 18, 2008
"For the first time in my adult life I am proud of my country."
(Age 44)

Barack Obama
March 9, 2008
"We are no longer a Christian nation - at least not just."

September 25, 2012
Remarks to the UN General Assembly
"The future must not belong to those who slander Islam."

Nancy Pelosi
March 9, 2010
"We have to pass the bill so that you can find out what is in it."

Hillary Clinton
January 23, 2013
"What difference, at this point, does it make?"

December 3, 2014
"...showing respect even for one's enemies, trying to understand
and insofar as psychologically possible, empathize with their
perspective and point of view."

Other Books by the Author

Novels:
Shades of Retribution
The Atlantis Crystal
She Waits in Atlantis
Return to Atlantis
America 20XX: The New World Order
666: Mark of the Beast
Death Drones: 2025

Children's Books:
Forest Trails and Fairy Tales
Wishing Wells and Broken Tales
Student Study Skills
American Heroes: Students Who Learn

Non-Fiction:
Simply Success
The Education Jungle
How to Learn
The Day America Died
Obama's Ring: The Seat of Satan
Managing Without Conflict
The Peer Pressure Monster
Denied 3 Times
The War on Christians
Who is the Antichrist
Islamic Two-Headed Beast
Islam Attacks the Whore